To m
Lisa, Micah, Dominic, Parker, and Zoe

D0822825

Contents

Contents

Chapter 6: Wolves and Humans

Acknowledgments

Much of the information for this book was gleaned from wolf research associated with the US Fish & Wildlife Service, state agencies, and universities. Thanks, all of you. The editors and authors of *Wolves: Behavior, Ecology and Conservation* deserve special acknowledgment. This book provided a veritable treasure trove of biological information on wolves and is recommended reading for those seeking to expand their knowledge of these creatures. Special thanks to wolf biologists Jon Rachael of the Idaho Fish & Game Department and Mike Jimenez of the US Fish & Wildlife Service for reviewing and commenting on the manuscript.

Introduction

My consciousness as a youngster encompassed two divergent worlds when it came to predators. On the family ranch in western Montana, my father trapped and killed predators—coyotes in particular—that infrequently attacked newborn calves during severe winters. I well remember a tiny calf we discovered one frigid February morning. A coyote had bitten its hindquarter. Through torn flesh I could see the shiny white bone of its hip joint. At that moment I hated coyotes. By fall the calf's wound healed, leaving only a ragged scar on its tough black hide.

Although antagonistic toward most predators and certain other species, my dad was possessed by an overall fascination with wildlife, an attitude that rubbed off on his children. Wildlife stories were among my favorite books I plucked from the shelves of the Three Forks School library. I especially loved tales of predators. I read with passion *Yellow Eyes,* a book about a mountain lion, and *Old One Toe,* a story of a fox. But my very favorite was *The Black Wolf of Savage River,* a 1959 fictional tale of an Alaskan wolf. When reading the books, I found myself rooting for the predators and against the hunters and trappers. In those moments I loved them all: coyotes, mountain lions, wolves, foxes, and bears.

While cross-country skiing in Yellowstone National Park in late winter 2000, I heard the howl of a wolf, mournful, deep, and very strong. Less than an hour later, my companions and I spotted three wolves at a distance. Since then I have observed wolves on numerous occasions, both in Yellowstone and other remote areas of Montana. They are fascinating and sometimes fearsome creatures. Neither the antipathy held by many ranchers and hunters toward wolves, nor the near-religious devotion many wolf advocates carry toward the creatures, can be justified, at least not in my mind.

In this book I hope to present a picture of wolves from the standpoint of natural history that focuses minimally on the social controversies surrounding these creatures. Informed management and conservation do not tolerate villains or celebrities in the world of wildlife. It is not appropriate to view wolves in either light. It is my hope that the future of wolves and humans in the United States will soon enter an era where these iconic predators are afforded no more or no less respect than other carnivores and their prey.

CHAPTER 1

Names and Faces

Names and Visual Description

Wolf is the English name given to the largest species in the dog-like family of mammals, the canines. In the case of wolves, the common and scientific names are essentially equivalent, although they are derived from different languages. The common name, *wolf,* is Germanic in origin. The scientific, or Latin, name for the

Gray wolves may be black and nearly white, as well as their typical gray color. KEVIN RHOADES

wolf is *Canis lupus*. *Canis* refers to the animal's family, the canines. *Lupus* is the Latin word for "wolf." Thus, in reference to wolves, the common and scientific names are the same terms derived from different languages.

In North America, members of the *Canis lupus* species are most often described as wolves. However, in field guides and scientific literature, the species is more technically referenced by the term *gray wolf*. To a lesser extent these animals might also be known as timber wolves.

Gray wolves have the overall appearance of a large dog, somewhat similar to an oversize German shepherd or a malamute. When it comes to coloration, the name *gray wolf* is somewhat deceiving. Although most wolves have an overall grayish appearance, individual animals within various geographic regions and gene pools may be almost completely white to completely black. The "typical" gray wolf sports a grizzled gray coloration over its entire body, with darker highlights on the back, neck, and shoulders that yield to lighter tones on the lower rib cage, belly, and legs. Some wolves exhibit slightly reddish highlights in the lighter portions of their coats. On most animals, however, the paler part of their pelage is whitish or cream colored.

A wolf's legs appear long in relation to its body. This characteristic is more prominent in the summer, when the animal wears its shorter coat, than in the winter, when its fur is much longer. A wolf's tail is bushy and roughly one third the length of its body from the tip of its nose to the end of its rump, or slightly longer. A wolf with the common gray-grizzled appearance most often has a black tip on the end of its tail. When it is on the move, the wolf carries its tail straight out from its body.

A wolf's ears are erect and slightly rounded at the tips. Its black nose pad is more prominent than that observed on other canines; it measures more than 1 inch wide. A wolf's eyes are often described as orange or hazel in color with a distinct greenish cast. Framing a wolf's head is a ruff of longer hair that makes the face of the animal appear much larger than the underlying skull.

Unlike many other animal species that are given special terms for the two genders, terminology for the wolf sexes is very simple. Male wolves are referred to as males, and female wolves are called females. Their offspring, like the babies of domestic dogs, are known as pups.

Related Species in North America

Gray wolves share temperate and arctic regions of North America with six other canine species: coyotes, red foxes, swift foxes, kit foxes, gray foxes, and red wolves. Given the extreme difference in size between wolves and foxes, it's unlikely that a reasonably educated observer would ever mistake a fox for a wolf. Tiny kit foxes usually weigh a mere five pounds or less. Even the largest fox species, the red fox, is much small than the wolf. At around fifteen pounds, large red foxes are still four times smaller than a small adult wolf. What's more, all the North American fox species exhibit a coloration that is very different from gray wolves.

Differentiating gray wolves from coyotes and red wolves, however, isn't quite as simple. Despite their smaller size, each of these two species can be easily confused with gray wolves.

The most obvious difference between a coyote and a gray wolf is its size. In terms of weight, coyotes usually weigh from twenty-five to forty-five pounds, roughly half the size of an adult wolf of modest proportions. An adult wolf stands about 2.5 feet tall at the shoulder; a coyote is only 1.5 feet tall. But unless the two species are observed in proximity to one another (an unlikely occurrence) or the observer has had ample opportunities to view both species separately, the untrained eye can easily confuse a coyote for a wolf.

Beyond size, what's the best way to tell the two species apart? In some cases identification is quite obvious. Gray wolves that sport black coats or are nearly white can be distinguished from coyotes based on color. But trained observers can positively identify animals of the two species that are similar in color by paying attention to differences in size and other physical features.

Red foxes and coyotes are smaller canines that share ranges with wolves in some areas.
LISA DENSMORE

Red wolves that live in the southeastern United States are midway in size between gray wolves and coyotes. Steve Hillebrand, courtesy USFWS

When it runs, a wolf carries its tail straight out behind its body. A coyote, by contrast, keeps its tail low, sometimes between its legs. In relation to the rest of its face, the black nose pad appears smaller on a coyote than on a wolf. A coyote's ears appear slightly larger and more pointed than those of a gray wolf. However, this feature is somewhat variable depending upon the time of year, the latitude in which the animal lives, and individual variations. Viewed head-on, a wolf's face is described by some biologists as more blocky and square, while a coyote's face is narrow and triangular.

5

Gray wolves also share the North American continent with red wolves, a species aptly described by some naturalists as appearing as a cross between a gray wolf and a coyote. In both size and appearance, red wolves have the look of a gray wolf–coyote intermediary. It is believed that red wolves became extinct in the wild by 1980. In 1973 the US Fish & Wildlife Service began a captive breeding program for the species. Since 1987, red wolves have been reintroduced in the southeastern United States, with the highest concentration of animals occurring in North Carolina. Because current red wolf and gray wolf ranges in the United States are separated by many hundreds of miles and geographical obstacles, it's not likely to confuse the species, at least not yet. However, the interactions between gray wolves, coyotes, and red wolves represent a fascinating, yet puzzling peek into the workings of nature, our next topic of discussion.

Subspecies

Worldwide, gray wolves have been separated into at least thirty-two subspecies by biologists at various times in history. Of those subspecies, twenty-four have historically been identified in North America. Most of the subspecies are associated with particular habitats and regions in which they live (or have lived). For example, the Alaskan tundra wolf, *Canis lupus tundrarum*, roams along the Arctic coast of northern Alaska. An extinct subspecies, the Mogollon mountain wolf, *Canis lupus mogollensis*, is named for the native Mogollon people of New Mexico and Arizona, the region it inhabited until its extinction in the early part of the twentieth century.

Many wildlife biologists in recent times have proposed reducing the number of North American subspecies of gray wolf from two dozen to five.

The Mexican gray wolf, *Canis lupus baileyi*, is the most easily identifiable, due to its current isolation from other wolves. According to the US Fish & Wildlife Service, the Mexican gray wolf "is the smallest, southern-most occurring, rarest, and most

Mexican gray wolves are the smallest subspecies of gray wolves. Shutterstock

genetically distinct subspecies of gray wolf in North America." Prior to the settlement of the American Southwest by Europeans, Mexican gray wolves occupied vast regions of Texas, New Mexico, Arizona, and Mexico. Conflict with livestock interests prompted widespread killing of these wolves in the early 1900s. By the middle of the twentieth century, Mexican gray wolves had been essentially extirpated from the United States and severely reduced in Mexico.

The smallest subspecies of gray wolf, Mexican gray wolves range in weight from approximately fifty to eighty pounds, are 5 to 6 feet in length (including the tail), and about 2.5 feet tall at the shoulder. Mexican gray wolves are quite similar in size to German shepherd dogs. Unlike other gray wolf subspecies, Mexican gray wolves do not exhibit nearly white or nearly black color phases. Rather their coats are a mix of gray, black, buff, and reddish brown. The primary prey species of Mexican gray wolves include elk, mule deer, and whitetail deer, along with other smaller mammals. Like larger subspecies of gray wolves, the Mexican gray wolf is capable of, and sometimes does, kill livestock, such as young calves and sheep.

In 1977 the United States and Mexico began a cooperative captive breeding program with Mexican gray wolves. Because this wolf was listed as an endangered species in the United States in 1976, the goal of this program was to reestablish a viable population in the American Southwest. In 1998, Mexican gray wolves bred and reared in captivity were released in the Blue Range Wolf Recovery Area in the Apache National Forest in eastern Arizona. Offspring from this initial reintroduction, and captive-reared wolves released in subsequent years, now roam across mountainous portions of southeastern Arizona and southwestern New Mexico in the Apache and Gila National Forests. The White Mountain Apache Tribe became a formal partner in Mexican gray wolf recovery efforts in 2002. Wolves have been released and now occupy portions of the Fort Apache Indian Reservation. A decade after the recovery program for the Mexican gray wolf began, approximately fifty wolves were living in New Mexico and Arizona.

Northwestern wolves, like this large one in Yellowstone National Park, often weigh more than one hundred pounds.

Another subspecies, the eastern wolf or eastern timber wolf, *Canis lupus lycaon,* occupies southeastern Canada. These wolves are also known as eastern Canadian wolf, eastern Canadian red wolf, eastern gray wolf, and Algonquin wolf. These wolves are found in Algonquin Provincial Park, Ontario, and other adjacent regions. Historically the eastern wolf ranged across the northeastern United States and westward toward the Great Lakes.

West of the range of the eastern wolf, the plains wolf or Great Plains wolf, *Canis lupus nubilis,* historically occupied a massive range consisting of the interior portions of the United States, westward through the Rocky Mountains to the northern Pacific Coast. The plains wolf also ranged along the mountains of Canada's Pacific Coast and into northeastern Canada toward Hudson Bay. Currently the plains wolf is found in the Great Lakes area of northern Minnesota, Wisconsin, and Michigan. At the present time the plains wolf is the most abundant subspecies inhabiting the continental United States. This subspecies is sometimes called the buffalo wolf, in reference to one of its historic prey species on the Great Plains.

To the north and west of the plains wolf's historic range lies the range of the northwestern wolf or Rocky Mountain wolf, *Canis lupus occidentalis,* also known as the Alaskan wolf or Mackenzie Valley wolf. The historic and current range of this wolf lies primarily in the mountainous areas of western Canada and Alaska. Its historic and current range also juts southward into the contiguous United States in northern Montana, Idaho, and Washington. When wolves were reintroduced into Yellowstone National Park and central Idaho from Canada in 1995 and 1996, members of the northwestern subspecies were chosen. Wolves transplanted in 1995 were captured in an area east of Jasper National Park near Hinton, Alberta, a region roughly 550 miles north of Yellowstone National Park. Animals relocated from Canada in 1996 came from the Williston Lake area of British Columbia, about 750 miles north of the Yellowstone release site. Northwestern wolves were chosen from these areas because of

Arctic wolves live in the far north and are usually white or nearly white in color. Shutterstock

SPECIES, SUBSPECIES: DOES IT MATTER?

Distinguishing one species from another is an easy matter, right? A black bear is not a mountain lion. A bald eagle is not a mallard. Anyone with normal vision can take a quick look at these animals and easily tell that they're different species.

However, differentiating species of more closely related animals isn't quite so simple. Even though they look quite different, grizzly bears and polar bears can mate and produce fertile offspring. Does that make them the same species?

Some biologists would actually argue "yes." The only reliable way to differentiate species, they reason, is by separating animals that are so genetically dissimilar that they cannot reproduce or if they do (such is the case with the horse and donkey) that their offspring are infertile. For the purposes of this discussion, let's call this the "fertile offspring" theory of species identification, the belief that all animals that can theoretically mate and produce fertile offspring belong to the same species no matter how different they look or where they live.

Other biologists argue that even among closely related animals that can practically or theoretically reproduce, species can be differentiated based on factors such as physical characteristics (size, color, and so on), differing behaviors, geographic distribution, and, more recently, variations in genetic makeup, or DNA. Thus, even though polar bears and grizzly bears can mate and rear fertile cubs, the differences in appearance, normal geographic distribution, and DNA are enough to maintain them as separate species. Let's call this the "differing biological factors" theory of species identification.

When it comes to wolves, these competing theories yield very different outcomes. From the standpoint of the fertile offspring theory, coyotes, gray wolves, and red wolves all belong to the same species and at best are subspecies. Applying the differing biological factors theory yields conundrums and controversy. Red wolves have genetic markers of both wolves and coyotes, leading some biologists to conclude that they are simply a geographically isolated wolf-coyote hybrid. Eastern wolves also carry coyote genetic markers, and with the expansion of the coyote's range in the northeastern United States and southeastern Canada, will likely experience more genetic influence from coyotes in the future. However, some biologists also argue that there is enough genetic and geographic difference between eastern wolves and other gray wolves that they should be classified as a distinct species altogether. In 2011, the US Fish & Wildlife Service proposed designating the eastern wolf as a separate species (*Canis lycaon*), separate from gray wolves (*Canis lupus*) and red wolves (*Canis rufus*).

What does it matter? Without going into too much detail, the controversy surrounding species and subspecies designations for wolves can be extremely important legally. Whether a population of animals is a species or a subspecies can have critical ramifications for the amount of protection it is afforded and its management under the Endangered Species Act (ESA). Thus, a potentially contentious political dimension to biology enters the picture. Wolf preservation groups may lobby for a classification one way or another based on their interests, while opponents may argue differently.

Species and subspecies designations do matter, at least in terms of endangered or threatened wildlife. When it comes to wolves, the definitions may prove to be an uneasy mix of politics and debatable biological postulates.

their excellent health and occupation of habitat that closely resembles that of Yellowstone Park and central Idaho.

Given ample prey, northwestern wolves grow quite large. Members of this subspecies range in weight from around 85 to 115 pounds and stand nearly 2.5 feet at the front shoulder, which is considerably larger than the three subspecies previously described. Exceptionally large northwestern wolves may weigh up to 145 pounds. In Alaska, northwestern wolves may inhabit territories as large as 600 square miles. Northwestern wolves are usually gray or black in color, with some animals exhibiting an intermediary pelage between gray and black with a markedly bluish appearance.

Arctic wolves, *Canis lupus arctos,* occupy the northernmost dwelling of any gray wolf subspecies. Sometimes called polar wolves or white wolves, this species roams barren, frozen environments primarily north of the Arctic Circle. Several adaptations help these wolves survive in one of the harshest environments on the planet. Their muzzles, legs, and ears are fairly short, helping them retain body heat. Fur between the pads of their feet and exceptionally long, thick fur further insulate them from extremely cold temperatures that may plunge to -70 degrees Fahrenheit. Arctic wolves have white coats that blend with their snowy surroundings, enhancing their ability to stalk prey. They primarily prey upon musk oxen and arctic hares. They also consume caribou, birds, lemmings, and sometimes seals. Prey is much less abundant in the Arctic than in other places gray wolves live, which means arctic wolves may maintain territories in excess of 1,000 square miles.

Physical Characteristics

Like other species that occupy a wide range of latitudes and habitats, wolf sizes vary considerably. Small members of the southern-dwelling Mexican wolf subspecies may weigh a modest fifty pounds, while exceptionally weighty specimens of the northwestern subspecies occasionally triple them in bulk. How large can wolves become? A wolf weighing 175 pounds was killed in Alaska in 1939.

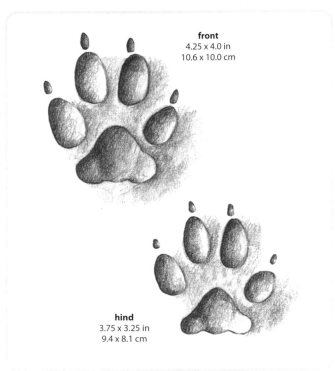

front
4.25 x 4.0 in
10.6 x 10.0 cm

hind
3.75 x 3.25 in
9.4 x 8.1 cm

Wolves have very large feet compared to similar-size domestic dogs. According to the National Zoo in Washington, D. C., a captive wolf weighing sixty pounds has paws similar in size to a one hundred-pound domestic dog. Adult wolf tracks average about 4.5 inches long by 3.5 inches wide, with prints of larger animals being notably bigger. The oversize feet of wolves allow them to run more easily in snow, serving somewhat like snowshoes.

CHAPTER 2 Range and Habitat

Historic Range

The regions inhabited by herbivores and carnivores follow different, but highly related patterns. Herbivores are found only where there are plants they find palatable and meet their nutritional requirements. Carnivores, on the other hand, live only where prey species that they can kill in sufficient numbers to sustain their existence are found. In some cases the range of its primary prey species largely determines a particular carnivore's range. The Canada lynx, for example, preys heavily on snowshoe hares. Snowshoe hares may constitute as much as 97 percent of a lynx's diet. Rarely does a lynx garner more than one third of

Current range of gray wolves in North America.

its diet from prey species other than hares. Thus the snowshoe hare's range largely determines the Canada lynx's range.

The ranges of less selective predators may overlap or correspond with numerous types of prey. Such is the case with wolves. Wolves generally glean most of their sustenance from mid-size to large ungulates such as moose, elk, caribou, musk ox, whitetail deer, mule deer, and bighorn sheep. Wherever a sufficient prey base of one or more of these herbivores exists, wolves are also likely to be found.

Describing the historic range of wolves in North America yields two interesting conclusions. First, one's estimation of historic ranges depends on whether or not the red wolf's range is included in the southeastern United States. Second, not all sources and the maps they produce of historic range agree. Assuming "historic range" refers to an animal's distribution prior to the European settlement of North America (around AD 1500), sources for determining historic range are highly variable. Archaeological materials, journals of trappers and other early explorers who encountered various animals, Native American histories, and other data all come into play when assessing the historic range of a particular creature. It is not an exact science.

Disagreement regarding the wolf's historic range is most prominent along areas of the Pacific Coast, most specifically California. Most sources exclude central and southern California from the historic range of wolves. Others show wolves absent from portions of Nevada, Arizona, Washington, and Oregon as well. However, historical records indicate wolves were found in the Sacramento Valley of central California. In 1918 a wolf killing was recorded in Los Angeles County, a county that lies along the Pacific Coast in the southwestern portion of the state.

When it comes to wolves, biologists agree that essentially every habitat in North America that contains large ungulates was inhabited by wolves, from mid-Mexico to the ice pack of the Arctic. Thus, if the historic range of "wolves" in North America includes both gray wolves and red wolves, these adaptable

Historically wolves roamed the deciduous forests of the central and eastern United States as well as the mountains and the plains.

carnivores essentially roamed across the entire continent with very few exceptions.

Historically, habitats that the public now perceive as being marginally associated with wolves held some of the greatest concentrations of these formidable predators. The seemingly innumerable herds of bison that grazed and galloped across the Great Plains, along with vast numbers of plains-dwelling elk, supported exceptionally large numbers of wolves. Many people today do not associate wolves with prairie habitats. However, given the enormous ungulate population on the prairies prior to European settlement, the rolling grasslands of the plains also held very high numbers of wolves.

Current Range

For the average person, determining the current range of wolves in North America involves some of the same problems as assessing the historic range. All sources do not agree. Even range maps from government agencies don't always show the same range. Wolves themselves are also making the endeavor more difficult. The animals are rapidly expanding their range in the western United States. Populations continue to disperse in the Great Lakes region as well. Some biologists believe wolves are also moving into the extreme northern regions of the Northeast.

When describing current wolf ranges, it's helpful to separate Alaska and Canada from the contiguous United States. Wolf populations in those areas have varied throughout modern history but are relatively stable, at least compared with the situation in the Lower 48. Wolves range across all of Alaska, inhabiting most of the major islands in the southeastern part of the state as well as the mainland. Most of Canada also holds wolves, from the frozen islands of the far north to the lush, coastal forests of British Columbia, including Vancouver Island. Wolves are not present on the Island of Newfoundland in eastern Canada. They are also absent in the southern portion of Saskatchewan, southeastern Alberta, and southwestern Manitoba.

In the contiguous United States, aggressive efforts by individuals and government agencies in the late 1800s and early 1900s eliminated wolves from virtually all of their historic range. Bounties (cash payments for killing a wolf) were instituted in many states as early as the 1840s. These bounties originally amounted to just a few dollars, but in a time when workers might toil for a dollar a day, the monetary incentive for hunting or trapping wolves was considerable.

The bounties offered by states were not a new invention. In 1630 the Massachusetts Bay Colony provided a bounty for settlers who killed wolves. Bounties were a very effective means of wolf elimination. For example, Montana's bounty law was enacted in 1884. In its first year, 5,450 wolf hides were presented to government officials as proof of wolf kills and processed for bounty payments. From 1900 to 1931, all but three counties in Montana reported bounty payments. With the exception of perhaps a few lone individuals, wolves were thought to be eliminated in the Treasure State in the 1930s. The timing of the wolf's demise in other states varied somewhat, but due to bounties, government-sponsored trapping and poisoning, along with incidental killing by ranchers and homesteaders, wolves were essentially eliminated from the Lower 48 by 1940.

However, one small segment of the gray wolf population persisted, despite such widespread elimination efforts. Wolves were never completely eliminated from the dense woods of northeastern Minnesota, although it is believed their population dropped to as low as a few hundred animals in the 1960s. During the extremely cold winter of 1948–1949, wolves actually recolonized a tiny portion of the United States. Isle Royale, Michigan, is the largest island in Lake Superior, measuring some 45 miles long by 9 miles across at its widest point. In the depths of this exceptional winter, an ice bridge formed between the island and the mainland of Canada, 15 miles away. Wolves crossed the ice, discovering a population of moose that had established itself on the island sometime after

1900. The moose probably came from Canada as well, perhaps swimming to the island.

Previously caught in a boom-and-bust population cycle in the absence of predators, moose populations on Isle Royale are now balanced by wolves. From a conservation standpoint, the timing of the wolves' arrival on Isle Royale was fortuitous. The island had been authorized as a National Park in 1931 by President Herbert Hoover "to conserve a prime example of North Woods Wilderness." Nine years later, Isle Royale National Park was established under the administration of Franklin Roosevelt. Arrival of the wolves less than a decade later indeed enhanced the "North Woods Wilderness" character of the national park.

Since its low point in the 1960s, when gray wolf numbers in the contiguous United States numbered a few hundred animals in northern Minnesota and around two dozen animals on Isle Royale, the population has now expanded to an excess of 6,200. The wolves of northeastern Minnesota, along with transients from Canada, have expanded their range to northern Wisconsin and Michigan's Upper Peninsula. Growth of wolf numbers in Wisconsin and Michigan has been very rapid. In the five years from 2005–2006 to 2010–2011 (winter population counts), the US Fish & Wildlife Service reported an increase in Wisconsin from 467 to 782 wolves and an increase in Michigan from 434 to 687 wolves. In both states, wolf numbers rose more than 50 percent in the five-year period. In Minnesota, gray wolf numbers have risen steadily in every decade since the 1960s and appear to have reached a stable to slightly increasing level of around 3,000 animals.

Minnesota wolves range across the northeastern third of the state, with their population expanding slightly south and westward. Large, lightly populated regions of national forest land comprise much of northeastern Minnesota and offer excellent habitat for wolves. As a rough estimate wolves are found northeast of a line beginning at the Minnesota–Wisconsin border approximately 60 miles north of Minneapolis, extending to the Minnesota–Canadian border about 30 miles east of the Minnesota–North Dakota border.

In Wisconsin, wolves are present mainly across the northern third of the state, an area with significant areas of State Forest and National Forest lands. A line drawn from Green Bay west and slightly north to the Governor Knowles State Forest on the Minnesota border roughly marks the southern boundary of Wisconsin's northern wolf population. Another population of wolves, located in the west-central portion of the state, ranges primarily throughout several protected areas in the region of the Necedah National Wildlife Refuge and Black River State Forest.

Michigan's wolves are primarily found in the Upper Peninsula, although wolf sightings in the lower portion of the state have increased in recent years. Wolves have been recorded in every county of the Upper Peninsula, with numbers typically higher in the west than in the east. The northernmost reaches of the Upper Peninsula, with their extreme winters and deep snows, limit whitetail deer densities, making it difficult for wolves to establish year-round territories during cycles of severe winters.

Where will Midwest wolves wind up next? One wolf traveled from Wisconsin to eastern Indiana. Another moved from Michigan to north-central Missouri. At least two lone wolves from the upper Midwest have made their way into Nebraska. Wandering wolves are most often young loners. If two of these individuals of mating age and differing sexes meet, it's possible they may mate and form a pack, leapfrogging a wolf population to a new area.

Since the reintroduction of gray wolves to Yellowstone National Park and central Idaho in 1995 and 1996, wolf numbers have grown rapidly in the northern Rocky Mountains.

The wolves reintroduced to central Idaho were released primarily at the edge of the Frank Church–River of No Return Wilderness. A total of thirty-five wolves were released in Idaho; thirty-one were released in Yellowstone. However, these were not the only wolves colonizing the Rockies in the 1990s. Wolves from Canada had moved into Montana's Glacier National Park

Wolf populations reintroduced to Yellowstone National Park in 1995 expanded rapidly.
BARRY O'NEILL, COURTESY NPS

and were slowly establishing themselves southward by the time wolves from Canada were transplanted to central Idaho and Yellowstone National Park. In more recent years other wolves from Canada have crossed into the contiguous United States and have been responsible, at least in part, for the establishment of a small population in Washington.

Currently at least 1,800 wolves roam the wild lands in portions of Wyoming, Montana, Idaho, Washington, and Oregon. Wyoming's wolves are found primarily in the northwestern part of the state, in the mountains of and around Yellowstone

National Park. For an approximation of Wyoming's wolf range, draw a line from the Montana border directly north of Cody to Lander. From Lander extend the line west and slightly south to the point where the borders of Wyoming, Idaho, and Utah intersect. The vast majority of Wyoming's wolves are found northwest of these lines.

In Montana, wolves are found in the greatest numbers in the mountainous areas in the western third of the state. For the purposes of approximation, a line can be sketched from the eastern boundary of Glacier National Park southward to Helena, then southwestward to Red Lodge. West of the line is where most of Montana's wolves roam. However, packs have also been established in several mountain ranges lying east of the line, including the Little Belt and Crazy Mountains.

Wolves range across most of central and northern Idaho, with additional packs claiming territories in the east-central portion of the state west of Yellowstone and Grand Teton National Parks. Roughly speaking, wolf range in Idaho lies north of a line drawn from Jackson to Boise, with the agricultural and flatter areas northwest of Idaho Falls containing few wolves.

Recently wolves have also come to occupy Washington and Oregon. Several packs have been established in the extreme northeastern corners of both states. In Washington at least one pack has taken up residence in the central part of the state in the Wenatchee Mountains northwest of Ellensburg. Another pack is now present in north-central Washington, in the Twisp River area southeast of North Cascades National Park.

Dispersals of lone wolves, usually young animals in search of a mate and new territory, have taken these creatures to locations far beyond their currently established range in the northern Rockies. A young male split from a pack in northeastern Oregon, traveled to the southern Cascade Range in southwestern Oregon, then crossed into California in 2011. The animal was photographed on a hunter's trail camera. It is presumed that prior to this incident a wild wolf had not made tracks in California since the 1930s. The last confirmed wolf sighting

Lone wolves that meet, mate, and form new packs often expand the range of wolves to new places. KEVIN RHOADES

Red wolves were reintroduced to the Alligator National Wildlife Refuge in North Carolina in 1987. STEVE HILLEBRAND, COURTESY USFWS

in southwestern Oregon was in 1946. In 2009 a young female wandered from Paradise Valley north of Yellowstone National Park to Colorado. Biologists believe her trip covered around 3,000 erratic miles and took about six months. Another wolf moved from the Yellowstone area to the Black Hills of South Dakota, where it was killed by a vehicle. Given the increasing population of gray wolves and the frequent dispersals of young animals, it's reasonable to predict that wolves will continue to expand their range into the southern Rocky Mountains and remote areas in western Washington, Oregon, and northern California. Many experts anticipate that gray wolves will continue to dispense east of the Rockies, but limited habitat and social conditions will prohibit the establishment of viable populations. However, wolf numbers in the northern Rocky Mountains may fluctuate significantly in the future due to hunting, trapping, disease, and changes in habitat conditions.

Mexican wolves (the gray wolf subspecies described in chapter 1) range over parts of New Mexico and Arizona. The wolves are currently found primarily on mountainous National Forest lands in southeastern Arizona and southwestern New Mexico. They also roam on the eastern portions of the White Mountain and San Carlos Apache Reservations in Arizona.

Red wolves are currently found in northeastern North Carolina. Animals from a captive breeding program were first released in the Alligator National Wildlife Refuge in 1987. Their population has expanded to cover roughly 1.5 million acres in northeastern North Carolina, including additional national wildlife refuges, a Department of Defense bombing range, and other private and public lands.

Wolf Habitat

Wolves can occupy essentially any type of habitat in which they can find sufficient prey. Although individual wolves can subsist on smaller quarry such as ground squirrels, hares, beavers, and birds, in most places the presence of wolf packs is dependent upon mid-size to large ungulates. Elk, moose, caribou, musk oxen, whitetail

Wolves can occupy nearly any habitat where they can find enough prey. KEVIN RHOADES

deer, and mule deer are primary prey species of wolves. They may also feed on other species such as bighorn sheep, pronghorn, and mountain goats.

Wolf habitat thus mirrors the range of their prey. From arid regions of the southwestern United States to the frozen tundra of northeastern Canada, wolf numbers tend to be highest in areas that hold the most abundant prey. They also tend to be the lowest in areas of high human population and activity. Wolves have lived and successfully reared young in a variety of areas including missile ranges and livestock pastures and near dumps. However, they're most comfortable in areas where they have limited contact with people.

CHAPTER 3 Abilities and Behavior

Over most of their range, gray wolves prey primarily on ungulates—large, hoofed animals. Thus, wolves require the speed, strength, and intelligence to effectively hunt and kill such creatures. If wolves were fleeter of foot than their prey species, it seems nature's balance would tip too much in favor of the predators and prey would become scarce. Compared to most of the creatures they hunt, wolves are evenly matched or slightly slower. A healthy whitetail deer can normally outrun a wolf, as can a mature elk.

Physical Abilities

That said, wolves are still quite fleet of foot. How fast are they? While researching this book, I encountered highly divergent estimates of wolf speed even from apparently credible sources. It appears that some "wolf fans" are as likely to inflate their favorite animal's abilities as is the admirer of a professional athlete. One source asserted wolves can run up to 45 miles per hour, a speed well in excess of reasonable estimates of any of their prey, with the exception of pronghorn, the fastest animal in North America. Most credible sources place the speed of wolves between 30 and 35 miles per hour, generally on par or slightly slower than their normal prey. One nationally recognized biologist notes that wolves seldom pursue their prey at speeds exceeding 25 miles per hour.

Within their territory wolves often move at speeds of 5 miles per hour or slightly faster for hours on end. Wolves are sometimes reputed as covering more than 100 miles per day when hunting, but such claims are exaggerated and are certainly based on extreme examples. Wolves with large territories have been recorded traveling 35 miles in a single night and 50 miles in a full day (twenty-four hours). Wolves with smaller territories, such as those on Michigan's Isle Royale, normally travel less than 10 miles per day while hunting in the winter.

In soft snow the narrow, pointed hooves of ungulates are more efficient than the broad pads on the feet of wolves.

Wolves may sprint over 30 miles per hour in pursuit of prey. Jim Peaco, courtesy NPS

The extra-large feet of wolves help them run more easily in deep or crusted snow.
JIM PEACO, COURTESY NPS

However, if the snow develops even a moderate crust, the wolf's spreading pads allow it to run efficiently on the surface, while the hooves of its prey break through the crust. This adaptation of gray wolves greatly enhances their predatory abilities in late winter, when freezing and thawing are most likely to create a crust on the surface of the snow. The sharp claws on a wolf's feet are not used as tools for grasping prey like those on a mountain lion, but they do serve an important purpose. They give the animal extra traction on hard soil, ice, and crusted snow.

Interestingly, the average pace of a hunting wolf can be easily matched by a fit, athletic human. American Indians of some groups ran down wolves in a game of endurance. Historical records also verify Europeans doing the same. In

1865 a Canadian in Saskatchewan ran down a wolf in a 100-mile effort that terminated when the worn-out wolf was killed by the pursuer's knife. Wolves possess both formidable speed and reasonable endurance, but in comparison to their prey, they excel at neither. Hunting success is more often a product of strategy and cooperation rather than speed or endurance, an aspect of wolf biology discussed in a later chapter.

Several features of the wolf's skull and dental structure are highly instrumental to its success as a predator. The teeth of a gray wolf are especially suited to delivering injurious bites to prey, then ripping and tearing at the meat once an animal has been killed. Wolves also have teeth that are specialized for crushing and cracking bones, which allows them to extract the nutritious marrow inside. From a hunting standpoint, the fangs or canine teeth of wolves are most important for subduing their prey. These teeth measure about 1 inch in length. They are very strong, sharp, and curved slightly backward to aid in holding prey. Toward the back of the wolf's mouth are another set of extremely important teeth known as the carnassials. These large, sharp teeth are used for slicing meat much like a pair of scissors shearing cloth. The function of these teeth is so critical that a wolf with cracked, infected, or excessively worn carnassials is at risk of starvation due to its inability to tear meat.

Several large and powerful muscles attached to the rear of its skull and jawbone close the wolf's jaws. Although the wolf's bite is not as strong as that of the slightly larger hyena, its jaws have enough power to crack bones from its prey. It has been estimated that a gray wolf's jaws exert significantly more force than those of a similar size domestic dog.

Wolves rely on several senses for hunting and communicating with their own kind. They have keen eyes, an uncanny sense of smell, and excellent hearing. Which of these senses is most important when hunting?

Many popular notions exist that say the wolf's sense of smell is its most highly developed and important sense. However, it is imperative to note that it is nearly impossible to construct and

A wolf's specialized teeth and exceptionally strong jaws are important predatory adaptations. SHUTTERSTOCK

control legitimate scientific experiments evaluating any of the wolf's sensory apparatuses. Biologists are thus forced to compare the sensory abilities of wolves with those of similar creatures, such as domestic dogs. Dogs can perceive and discriminate odors on a level that is one hundred to perhaps one million times more sensitive than that of the human nose. Wolves are presumed to have similar, if not greater, olfactory abilities than dogs. Several observations by researchers attest to the wolf's skill in detecting prey by scent. One biologist recorded wolves smelling three moose at a distance of 1.5 miles. Research on gray wolves in Minnesota indicates that they often use scent as a means of locating whitetail deer as prey. The *Canis lupus*'s sense of smell is also extremely important for communicating the territorial boundaries of packs, along with the sex and reproductive status of individual animals.

The wolf's eyes are quite different than human eyes. Wolves, like domestic dogs and various species of cats, have eyes that function well in both daylight and at night. Research on the vision of domestic dogs indicates that their eyes are more sensitive to motion and far more capable at differentiating variations in the color gray than human eyes are. Presumably the wolf's vision is likewise more sensitive. Human vision excels that of canines in its overall definition (clarity) and color distinction. At least one research study indicates that the wolf's vision may be sharper than that of domestic dogs. Suffice it to say that the wolf's enhanced ability to detect motion and excellent low-light vision serve it very well in detecting and pursuing prey. Research performed with captive coyotes indicates that eyesight is their most dominant sense when hunting. It is quite possible that wolves in open environments rely more heavily on their eyesight to detect prey, while those that inhabit forested regions favor their noses.

Wolf pups are born deaf, but they attain adult-level hearing capabilities within three weeks. The erect ears of a wolf point toward sounds the animal finds interesting. Research specific to wolves' hearing is absent, but most biologists believe they have hearing capabilities similar to domestic dogs—more acute than humans, but not exceptional in relation to other mammals.

A wolf's eyes are especially suited to detecting motion and function remarkably well in low light. KEVIN RHOADES

Wolves are definitely more sensitive to high-pitched noises than people are.

Compared to other clawed creatures such as bears and cats, wolves are unskilled in the use of their forepaws. Both grizzly bears and bobcats are adept at using their paws to manipulate objects or capture prey. Wolves, however, primarily use their teeth and jaws. Some researchers feel that the poor close-up vision of wolves is partly responsible for the limited use of their paws in sophisticated ways.

Vocal and Visual Communication

So varied and sophisticated are the vocal and visual communication of wolves that an entire book could be devoted to the subject. The

Wolves howl to communicate with each other and perhaps for other reasons. Lone wolves howl less frequently than members of a pack. SHUTTERSTOCK

intricate social web within a pack and between rival packs requires complex and subtle communication; without this communication, there would be excessively destructive conflict.

The wolf's iconic howl is the species' vocalization most recognized by humans. However, the actual role of howling in wolf communication is not as simple as many people believe. For example, most folks assume that howling is a territorial behavior. When a pack howls, it tells other wolves to stay away. Biologists testing this theory have played recordings of wolf howls in the vicinity of a pack to see how it would respond. Packs that did not return the recorded howls with vocalizations of their own usually moved away. Packs that howled back stood their ground. Wolves defending a kill or protecting pups often howl

Wolves communicate with body language such as bared teeth and snarls. Bared teeth may signal aggression or defensiveness. SHUTTERSTOCK aggressively. "Chorus howling," the scientific term that refers to multiple members of a pack howling at once, appears to serve an important function in maintaining a buffer between rival packs. Some theorists also believe that howling together strengthens the bond of wolves within a pack.

Lone wolves also howl, although not nearly as long or as frequently as those in a pack. Research indicates that the howls of single wolves last from around three to seven seconds. Rarely will the moan of a lone wolf last longer than twelve seconds. By contrast, the chorus of howls of gray wolves in a pack lasts from around thirty seconds to two minutes. Some biologists believe single wolves howl less frequently than packs to reduce their risk of being discovered and killed by a territorial pack.

Numerous authors have written eloquent descriptions regarding the howl of a wolf. The sound touches some people with sadness, others with strength and wildness. Despite our emotional reactions to the sound, exactly why wolves howl remains something of a mystery.

Along with howling, wolves communicate with one another (and sometimes other creatures) with noises similar to those of domestic dogs. Wolves bark, whine, whimper, and yelp as signs of submission. Barks indicate a wolf is disturbed or annoyed. They use a woofing sound to warn one another of danger. For example, a wolf may woof to announce a black bear approaching the den. Pups respond to woofs by retreating to cover or the den. Wolves may switch from a woof to a bark as a threat comes closer. Much like a barking dog, wolves may either attack or flee, depending on their perception of the danger represented by an intruder. Growls and snarls are other noises wolves make that signal aggression and conflict. These sounds are usually emitted in dominance displays and defensive situations.

Gray wolves also use body language to communicate, which provides a visual signal of their intentions. Again, much of the wolf's body language parallels that of the domestic dog. In an aggressive or defensive situation, the hairs on a wolf's neck and back may become erect. It may pull back its lips and snarl.

Wolves also signal submission through body language. When approaching a dominant member of the pack, a subordinate wolf may maintain a low crouch, with its ears back and tail lowered. Submissive wolves also wag their tails and attempt to lick or nuzzle dominant animals.

Pack Structure and Dynamics

Wolf packs are generally composed of a breeding pair and their offspring. New packs are formed when lone wolves of the opposite sex become pairs and produce pups. Younger members of the pack are usually one to three years old. Typically, young wolves disperse from the pack in their first year or two of life. The dominant male and female within a pack are commonly known as alphas in the public vocabulary, although this term is rarely used

Disruption within a wolf pack's social structure can increase conflict among members of the pack. KEVIN RHOADES

AN INFAMOUS ALPHA

On an early morning in May 2000, wolf observers in Yellowstone National Park found a badly mauled female wolf. The alpha female of the Druid Peak pack, she had been attacked by members of her own pack and would soon succumb to her wounds. Known as #40F, she had previously ruled the Druids with iron teeth, viciously harassing her sister and two daughters, disrupting their denning attempts, and "disciplining" the subordinates with a ferocity not normally seen in wolf packs. Researchers speculate that the aggressive, seemingly cruel behavior of #40F was instrumental in causing her mother and another sister to abandon the pack.

During the time #40F reigned as alpha female of the Druids, the pack reflected some of her super-aggressive character. The pack was responsible for killing coyotes, other wolves, and even mountain lions that trespassed in its territory. Evidently, #40F's subordinate sister and daughter finally had had enough, turning on the ruthless matriarch in an uprising that left her dead.

In the world of wolves, like humans, there are extreme personalities. Just as an individual's character cannot be completely assessed from a single act of selfishness or generosity, a species cannot be characterized by an individual or small group. Observers who saw only the Druid Peak pack might conclude that social dynamics among wolves are much more violent than they actually are. Sound biology is based on multiple observations of many animals in various habitats and contexts. The behavior and death of #40F is a good reminder of this principle and also underscores that in the natural world, individual animals sometimes exhibit behaviors that are very different from the norms for their species.

by wolf biologists. In conflict with other pack members, they are dominant. As the alphas age, they may be challenged by younger members of the pack. In the case of females, an alpha that is successfully challenged by a younger wolf may stay with the pack, although displaced alphas are often driven away or even killed. In at least two cases in Yellowstone National Park, dominant females have been killed by rival females within the pack.

For the most part wolf packs behave harmoniously, like the extended family that they are. Cooperation and camaraderie are much more normal than conflict. Conflict is most likely to occur when there is a major disruption in the pack's structure. Alpha members, both male and female, may be killed when hunting, by rival packs or by humans. When this happens, a wolf from outside the pack may join and take up the role of an alpha, or a formerly subordinate member might gain the position. In either case, such disruption within a pack can cause a period of tension and conflict. Once leadership has been reestablished, the pack normally returns to its harmonious way of living.

CHAPTER 4 Wolves and Other Animals

Wolves are considered apex predators. Yet the prey of gray wolves consists of other animals and food sources beyond the large ungulates that make up the bulk of their diet in most locations.

Wolves and Their Prey

Prey Species

Arctic wolves prey upon arctic hares. In some places, beavers represent a significant source of nutrition for wolves. Wolves may also opportunistically kill juvenile snowshoe hares and other rabbits, along with young birds and other smaller creatures, mostly in the summer. Around den sites, wolves often hunt for even smaller mammals, such as mice and ground squirrels. In Alaska, they sometimes eat spawning salmon.

Wolves may also scavenge the carcasses of dead animals. In Yellowstone National Park wolves occasionally dine upon elk and other animals struck and killed by vehicles. Wolves targeting these carcasses have also been struck and killed by vehicles. Wolves sometimes eat berries and fruits in the summer, perhaps to gain specific nutrients. Like domestic dogs, wolves will also

scat
4.0 x 1.25 in
10.0 x 3.2 cm

eat grass to induce vomiting, which may assist in expelling internal parasites or hair from the digestive tract.

But across the vast majority of their habitat, wolves meet their nutritional requirements by preying on weighty ungulates, of which bison are the largest. Bison represent occasional prey for wolves in Yellowstone and Grand Teton National Parks in the contiguous United States and in a few isolated areas in Canada. Wolves seldom attempt to kill a healthy adult bison. Instead, in the winter they actively target old and weak animals. In the summer they harass groups of bison in an attempt to separate vulnerable young from the herd. Bison represent a very small percentage of wolf prey, even where they are abundant.

Wolves also prey upon moose, another large ungulate. Moose roam over most of Alaska and Canada, where they are an important prey species for wolves. In the contiguous United States, wolves prey upon moose in the northern Rocky Mountains and the Great Lakes region. Most biologists believe that moose pose the greatest risk to attacking wolves of any of their prey. Moose are surprisingly quick and agile. A wolf struck by a direct or incidental blow from a moose's hoof during a predation attempt may be severely injured or killed.

Moose, elk, and whitetail deer are common prey species for wolves in the United States.
LISA DENSMORE (TOP)

Large and clumsy-looking, musk oxen are an important source of prey for arctic wolves. Musk oxen use their herds as a defensive tactic against wolves. The young are bunched toward the middle, with adults facing outward in a circle. The long, curved horns of the musk oxen on the outside of the circle can impale an attacking wolf. Wolves can most efficiently kill musk oxen by creating enough confusion in the herd that the oxen run, making it possible for wolves to target a single animal.

Elk and caribou are middle-size prey animals for wolves. Wolves prey upon caribou in Alaska and Canada. Although animals may occasionally drift into the northern United States from western Canada, few, if any, caribou are prey for wolves in the Lower 48. Elk roam the Rocky Mountains of the contiguous United States and western Canada, with some animals also present in Alaska. Elk and caribou are the favorite prey of wolves in many of the areas they inhabit.

Of the smaller ungulates that wolves target, whitetail deer are the most common. Wolves in much of southern Canada, the Great Lakes region, and the Rocky Mountains frequently prey upon whitetail deer. Other smaller ungulates wolves prey upon are mule deer and bighorn and Dall sheep. Wolves also may occasionally kill mountain goats and pronghorn.

In agricultural areas and where ranchers graze livestock in mountainous regions, wolves sometimes kill domestic animals such as cattle, horses, sheep, and goats. Wolves that learn to prey upon livestock, whether individual animals or packs, often develop a preference for this prey. They chase and test domestic animals for signs of weakness and vulnerability, just like they do with wild animals. Individuals or packs that repeatedly kill livestock may be shot by ranchers or wildlife agents to protect the livelihood of agricultural families.

Hunting Strategies

Wolves use a variety of hunting strategies to take down their prey. Their methods may change in relation to the number and

Wolves stalk as close as they can to their prey before making a rush to attack. KEVIN RHOADES

skill of wolves in the pack, the size of the prey and the habitat, and the conditions of the day.

The first thing hunting wolves must do is locate their prey. Scent, sight, and sound are all important means of finding a meal. Although sound is a less obvious method than scent and sight, vocal clues to the location and type of prey can greatly enhance a wolf's chances of making a kill. For example, the bleating of a young elk separated from a herd not only alerts wolves to its whereabouts, but also gives a strong indication of its vulnerability. Biologists also note that like human hunters, wolves sometimes have lucky encounters with their intended prey. For example, a wandering wolf may happen upon a mother grouse with a clutch of a half-dozen, easy-to-catch chicks or fortuitously encounter a lame elk while returning to a den site.

Locating prey that they can successfully kill occupies much of a wolf's life. Researchers have found that during winter, 25 to 50 percent of a wolf's time is spent in search of prey. Wolves on the hunt generally walk or trot in a single file, but they may spread out in forested or brushy areas, a strategy that increases their odds of discovering or flushing creatures in places where it is difficult for them to see at a distance.

Usually when wolves spot prey, they attempt to get as close to it as possible before attempting a chase. They use trees, vegetation, ravines, rocks, and other natural sight barriers to approach their prey without being detected. Wolves become very excited while stalking prey, moving more quickly and wagging their tails. They may approach small prey uneducated to the wiles of predators and thus easily captured, such as very young ungulates and hares, more directly once they spot them.

After closing the gap as much as possible, wolves sprint forward in a rush toward their prey. However, not all members of a pack may participate in the rush. Wolves sometimes use an ambush strategy, where some members of the pack circle behind the prey and wait to intercept it while other wolves make the rush.

An animal's reaction to the rush of hunting wolves often determines its survival. Large, strong creatures such as moose and elk may stand their ground. If they do, wolves often spend some time harassing them, attempting to bite at their flanks and haunches. Animals that respond with vigorous, well-aimed kicks or sweeping antlers are normally left alone after a short period of testing. Bison and musk oxen may refuse to run and may even become aggressive in driving wolves away. Whitetail deer are much smaller than moose or bison, but deer that stand their ground may also repel the attack of a wolf pack.

Whether targeting a single animal or a herd, wolves want to make their prey run. Oftentimes a fleet creature, such as a deer, will simply outrun the wolves. If the wolves can keep up with a single animal, they usually attempt to bite at its hindquarters and sides. Puncture and slashing wounds caused by a wolf's fangs slow and weaken the animal due to a loss of blood. During chases that follow a zigzagging course, some members of the wolf pack may run diagonally to cut off the flight of their prey. Wolves may also attempt to bite and hold the nose of a fleeing animal, hoping to bring it down. Not all animals that lose their footing during a chase are doomed, however. In Yellowstone National Park, I once saw a cow elk pulled down by two wolves regain her footing. Although badly wounded, she managed to outrun the wolves to a river where she found safety standing in deep water between two strong currents that the wolves were unable to swim without being swept downstream. Did she get away? Although I didn't see the final outcome, a very large grizzly bear was walking along the riverbank in the direction of the elk, about a quarter of a mile away. I suspect that the job begun by the wolves may have been finished by the bear.

When targeting a herd of creatures, wolves normally single their efforts upon young, weak, or wounded animals. Sometimes wolves will simply run alongside the herd, a strategy that biologists believe is designed to identify easier targets. Wolves do not always prey on just the young, weak, and injured, however. In areas of high wolf densities, where more vulnerable animals are often eliminated from the herds, wolves can and do kill healthy adult animals.

Wolves often target old or weak animals, like this bison in Yellowstone National Park.
COURTESY NPS

Despite gray wolves' position as apex predators, their percentage of success in predation attempts is quite low. Many factors influence these predators' success rates as hunters. A study of wolf predation attempts in a national park found that their success was almost twice as high during a severe winter than during the subsequent mild one. Research on Isle Royale indicates that wolves are successful in less than 10 percent of their predation attempts on moose. Interestingly, on a per-wolf basis, wolves hunting singly, in pairs, or in small packs are more successful hunters than members of large packs. Packs with numerous individuals often contain many young members, whose hunting skill and strength are inferior to adult wolves.

Wolves and Other Predators

Wolves share their range with numerous other predators, yet the number of other carnivores with which they compete directly for prey is quite small. Grizzly bears sometimes hunt the same prey as wolves, yet with the exception of targeting young animals in the spring, grizzly bears are seldom in direct competition with wolves. The same is true of coyotes. Packs of coyotes infrequently kill adult deer, but they can easily take down fawns, prey also prized by wolves. However, for most of the year coyotes are after much smaller prey. Mountain lions may be the predator with which wolves compete most directly for food. These large cats routinely prey upon deer and elk, two species that also comprise a significant portion of the wolf's diet in many habitats.

Grizzly bears are the only predator in North America that can successfully dominate a pack of wolves in a physical confrontation on a regular basis. In Alaska and Canada, and locations in the contiguous United States such as Glacier and Yellowstone National Parks, grizzly bears and wolves may regularly come into conflict. Most confrontations occur at kill sites, where a grizzly bear attempts to steal a carcass from wolves or vice versa. Researchers in Yellowstone National Park have concluded that adult grizzly bears are usually successful in defending or usurping a kill from wolves. When grizzlies investigate den sites, wolves are

Adult grizzly bears are large and strong enough to chase wolves from a kill. LISA DENSMORE

most often successful in driving them away. Wolves kill grizzly bear cubs on rare occasions, and adult grizzlies have also been known to kill wolves.

With the exception of grizzly bears, wolf packs dominate in conflicts with other predators, sometimes actively seeking and killing competitors within their territory. Wolf packs are known to kill mountain lions and black bears, occasionally attacking the bears in their dens. However, there are also documented instances of both mountain lions and black bears killing wolves.

Smaller carnivores are also at risk from wolves. Prior to their reintroduction into Yellowstone National Park, packs of coyotes were "top dogs." The fourteen wolves released in Yellowstone in 1995 were documented killing at least thirteen adult coyotes in their first winter. In the first three years after the return of the wolf, the territories of coyote packs shifted and splintered. Dominance hierarchies were disrupted due to the elimination of alpha members by wolves, causing some coyote packs to disintegrate and others to contract in numbers. The northern portion of Yellowstone, often referred to as the northern range, saw a 50 percent reduction in the coyote population within three years of the wolf's reintroduction. In some places representing core areas inhabited by wolf packs, coyote numbers plummeted by 90 percent. For some species of ungulates, the change was positive. The park's pronghorn numbers increased, as fewer fawns were killed by coyotes.

Wolves are also known to kill other small carnivores such as red foxes. Researchers in Denali National Park, Isle Royale, and Wood Buffalo National Park in Alberta have documented red fox kills by wolves. However, although smaller canines like red foxes and coyotes may die at the jaws of wolves, they also benefit from their larger cousins. Coyotes routinely scavenge on carcasses of animals killed by wolves, as do other creatures such as foxes, ravens, and magpies.

Parasites and Diseases
Parasites and diseases that infect domestic dogs often afflict wolves, too. Internal parasites, such as roundworms,

tapeworms, and hookworms are commonly found in wolves. Heartworms have also been documented in wild wolves. Generally, wolves can tolerate low to moderate infestations of these parasites without negative effects. However, severe cases of intestinal parasites can weaken wolves, diminishing their ability to hunt.

External parasites, including ticks and fleas, are also often found on wolves. Mange, a skin affliction caused by a mite, can cause wolves to lose their hair, creates scabs, and causes intense itching. Researchers have documented wolf deaths due to

ISSUES & WOLVES

COMPETITION WITH HUMAN PREDATORS

Wolves and grizzly bears may fight over a carcass, but the predator with which wolves may compete the most directly is the *homo sapien*. Growing wolf numbers in the Rocky Mountains have significantly reduced elk numbers in some places. Elk meat is as prized by many people as it is by wolves. In many Western communities, hunting is an important historical and cultural activity. Some families in rural areas depend on wild game as a source of lean, healthy red meat that can often be acquired more cheaply than beef from the supermarket.

Many hunters would like to see fewer wolves and more game animals. Many wildlife advocates don't feel that wolf numbers should be reduced through hunting or any other means. As wolf management in the United States is increasingly turned over from the federal government to states, striking a balance between the interests of two carnivores, wolves and humans, may prove to be a difficult endeavor.

mange in Yellowstone National Park, Minnesota, Wisconsin, and elsewhere. The hair loss caused by mange can be so severe that infected animals are unable to hunt and die from starvation and exposure during the winter.

Wolves are also susceptible to a number of diseases, including rabies. A severe rabies outbreak once infected a number of wolf packs in Alaska, causing a severe reduction in their population. While rabies may cause temporary setbacks to wolf numbers in local areas, its effect on long-term populations is probably minimal. Parvovirus (parvo), another canine virus that is most devastating to pups, can also temporarily inhibit wild wolf populations. Canine distemper is yet another disease contracted by gray wolves. Yellowstone wolves have suffered from bouts of distemper that have seasonally reduced their numbers.

CHAPTER 5 Reproduction and Young

The Mating Season

The mating season of wolves normally occurs from January to April, depending on the latitude where the animals are found. Wolves living in southern locations breed sooner than those living in the north. In Montana, and similar latitudes in the contiguous United States, gray wolves mate from mid to late February. Red wolves in North Carolina begin mating around the first of February, but females may conceive a litter of pups in March as well. The Mexican wolves of New Mexico and Arizona breed from late January to early March. Arctic wolves breed the latest. The breeding season for this northern subspecies generally occurs in April.

Courtship and mating among wolves follow one of several patterns. In the most typical scenario, the alpha male and female mate to produce young within a pack. However, subordinate females may also mate with the alpha male and produce a litter. Young produced by two females within the same pack is uncommon. This rare occurrence usually happens in places where prey is abundant, making it possible for members of the pack to nourish two litters of pups. In most cases when two females within a pack produce offspring, the mothers are either sisters or an older alpha female and her daughter. Wolf researchers have documented at least one occurrence among arctic wolves where an alpha female that advanced past reproductive age stayed with the pack while her daughter became the alpha male's mate and pup producer. Two sisters mating with the alpha is a temporary situation that seldom lasts more than a year or two. Eventually one of the females becomes dominant and the pack reverts to the normal pattern of one female birthing one litter of pups per year.

In captive wolves another male member of the pack may also mate with a female. However, the observed incidences

Courtship and breeding for gray wolves occur in late winter or early spring. SHUTTERSTOCK

of this behavior have occurred in packs that were highly disrupted (lacking one or both parent wolves), a situation that infrequently occurs in wild populations. Although it has been documented that subordinate males among wild wolves sometimes also breed, it is exceedingly rare. Under normal circumstances the alpha female interferes aggressively with subordinate females' attempts to court or mate with the alpha male. The alpha male is similarly intolerant of the mating behaviors of subordinate males.

Sometimes, however, these interference efforts are unsuccessful. On Isle Royale, after the dominant male of a pack disappeared, the alpha female accepted another mate. The new alpha male not only mated with the alpha female, but also with a subordinate female, even though she was chased from the pack by the alpha female several times.

How long do dominant male or female wolves retain their breeding status within a pack? Generally wolves that attain breeding status produce offspring for three to four years. However, researchers have observed wolves that have sired or birthed pups for as few as one year or as many as eight.

The mating season is the time when young females and males that have dispersed to new territories are most likely to meet and form a pair. If lone wolves meet, form a pair, and produce a litter of young, a pack is born. The meeting and mating of unrelated single wolves of the opposite sex is the most common means by which a new wolf pack is established. A male and a female that are unattached and become a breeding pair have an extremely difficult time establishing a territory and producing offspring in an area where wolves are already abundant. Under normal conditions packs are most readily formed in places where there is a robust prey base and few or no wolves to compete with the newly mated pair.

Prior to mating, reproductively capable wolves engage in a variety of territorial and courtship behaviors. Lone wolves of the opposite sex may meet and become associated as a pair at any time of the year. However, their courtship and mating behavior

Scent marking territory increases with paired wolves during the mating season. COURTESY NPS

will wait until late winter, the time at which other mated wolves in packs also prepare for breeding.

Territory marking via scratching the ground and urination increases among paired wolves before mating. Interestingly, newly mated wolves spend more time scent marking than established pairs. In packs the alpha male and female spend more time in close proximity, sometimes in seclusion from the rest of the pack. Researchers have observed that just prior to mating, wolf mates sleep within a yard of each other, much closer than they do after mating or at any other time of the year.

For some days prior to breeding, wolf pairs engage in other behaviors that are sometimes likened to the flirting between humans of the opposite sex who find one another attractive. The female may nuzzle the male, or the male may prance playfully toward the female. Prancing, nuzzling, playing, and sniffing are common courtship activities among wolves. But like courtship among people, a wolf of the opposite sex may be "turned off" or uninterested in the advances of another, sometimes playing hard to get. Another interesting parallel exists between human courtship and that of wolves: It is not always the most flirtatious female or the most aggressive male that is of most interest to wolves of the opposite sex. Wolves sometimes pay no attention to, or actively avoid, the overly enthusiastic advances of an animal of the other gender.

Pregnancy and Gestation

The gestation period (the amount of time between breeding and the birth of offspring) for wolves is not sharply defined. Most sources place the gestation period from sixty to sixty-five days. Looking for a figure easier to remember? If you define the gestation period of a wolf at nine weeks, you're right on target.

Once conceived, the pups' development proceeds rapidly. Within about three weeks, heartbeats of the developing pups can be detected. By the end of seven weeks, the fetuses have skeletons.

Pregnant females normally stay near the den where the pups will be birthed for several weeks before their arrival. At this time

Wolf dens are often dug in soft, sandy soil near water. KEVIN RHOADES

other members of the pack deliver food to the expectant mother. Den sites and construction follow some predictable patterns, but they exhibit a wide range of diversity depending on latitude, habitat, and the behavior of individual packs. Wolves often dig dens four to five weeks before the birth of a litter, but researchers have documented den digging as early as the previous autumn. All members of a pack may help with digging a den. Dens are excavated with their sharp, strong claws, much like a dog digging a hole in an attempt to burrow under a fence.

Of all the similar characteristics of wolf dens, proximity to water is perhaps the strongest. Wolf dens are typically located within 100 yards of a creek, river, or lake. Another highly predictable factor in the location of a den site is its position in the pack's home range. Wolves usually locate their dens in the interior of the pack's territory, where the pups have the least potential of encountering hostile individuals from a rival pack. Only rarely are dens found within half a mile of a pack's territorial boundary, the zone at which wolves are most likely to fight and be killed by members of competing packs.

Riverbanks and bluffs that afford southern exposure are often used as den sites. Wolves in many locations seem to prefer areas of soft or sandy soil, where it is easier to dig a den than in hard, stony ground. Dens may be dug under the roots of trees, too. Excavated dens may consist of a short tunnel that connects to a larger chamber or a simpler depression in the earth. In the far north, wolves sometimes dig a den in or through snowpack. Naturally occurring "dens" occasionally afford wolves the luxury of not digging a den at all. Arctic wolves often use caves or crevices in rocks as denning sites. Wolves in other areas may also use caves, along with hollow logs and abandoned beaver lodges. They might also simply enlarge a badger hole or another hole previously excavated by some other mammal.

Within a wolf pack's territory, there are often multiple den sites. Do females use the same den for birthing their pups every year? The short answer is no although female wolves generally prefer a known den. Packs may use a traditional denning site for over ten years. One wolf researcher has observed the traditional use of a den for fifteen consecutive years. While they may den in different sites from one year to the next, female wolves seem to prefer a known den. In a study of wild wolves in Minnesota, researchers found that most females (more than 80 percent) returned to a traditional denning site to birth their pups.

Birth

Wolf pups are birthed in a manner similar to domestic dogs. Many observers have likened the appearance of newborn wolf pups to the whelps of a German shepherd. Newborn wolves have fine, dark fur. They are born with their eyes closed and are deaf, presumably due to closed ear canals. Wolf pups arrive with small ears and blunt noses. Very shortly after birth they instinctively

Wolf pups are born blind, deaf, and helpless. The average litter size is five or six pups.
Kevin Rhoades

nuzzle their mother's belly. Upon encountering a nipple, their innate sucking reflex prompts them to nurse.

The average number of pups born in a litter is around five or six. Litters ranging from one to eleven have been observed. Several factors affect litter size. The age and health of the mother wolf is one of these. Females nearing the end of breeding age (around ten years old) tend to have fewer pups than younger females, as do those who are nutritionally stressed. In general, females tend to have larger litters where prey is abundant versus areas where the wolf pack must work much harder to sustain itself. Some experts believe that packs living in areas with a surplus of ungulate prey are more likely to have two young-producing females.

Compared to smaller wild canines such as coyotes and foxes, wolves birth fewer, larger pups. They range in weight from around ten ounces to slightly over one pound, with an average weight of fifteen ounces. Such creatures seem quite tiny, yet newborn wolf pups are at least four times larger than the newborn kits of a red fox.

Nurturing Pups to Adulthood

Biologists sometimes break the development from newborn to adult canine into four stages, a theory that is helpful in describing the maturation of young wolves. The *neonatal stage* refers to the period of time from birth until the pups open their eyes at roughly two weeks or a few days before. During this period the pups spend much of their time sleeping and nursing, often jumbled in a furry pile. Upon opening, the eyes of wolf pups are often blue, later transitioning to the greenish hazel common to grown wolves. However, a small number of wolf pups retain their blue eyes into adulthood.

The next period of development is known as the *transition stage*. This is a relatively short segment of development that occurs from the time wolf pups open their eyes until they gain enough strength and coordination to leave the den. During this stage their senses develop rapidly, especially those of touch and smell. Their muscles become stronger and more coordinated,

Female wolves may retrieve pups that wander from the den in their mouth. Pups may also be moved in this way from one den to another. KEVIN RHOADES

Wolf pups grow quickly and begin to follow the pack on hunting trips within four months of birth. KEVIN RHOADES

allowing them to walk or stumble about. The transition stage technically lasts from the time of eye opening until about three weeks of age.

At the end of the transition stage, wolf pups emerge from the den, where they encounter other members of the pack. This begins the *socialization stage,* when pups learn the correct ways to interact with the pack, their extended family. This stage ends when the pups reach about eleven weeks of age, at which time they are weaned from their mother's milk.

From three to five weeks of age wolf pups are still quite weak and uncoordinated, although their physical abilities develop quickly during this time. Pups learn to nurse their mother from a standing position. They seldom wander more than a few hundred yards from the den. If they do, the mother often retrieves them by carrying them in her mouth. By five weeks, pups have learned to follow their mother and other adult wolves in the pack. They may be moved from their birthing den to other dens within the pack's territory. Pups of this age have also learned to retreat to the den during bouts of nasty weather and to avoid potential predators.

After five weeks of age, wolf pups can generally digest small bits of solid food in addition to their mother's milk. Solid food is delivered to the pups through a unique behavior known as "lick up." When members of the pack return to the den after a successful hunt, they are met by pups that lick and nuzzle around the adults' mouths. This action prompts the adult wolf to regurgitate a portion of the contents of its stomach, which is then eaten by the pups. Both male and female members of the pack contribute to the pups' care in this way. As they age, young wolves learn to cache extra pieces of meat around the den site, which they may eat at a later time.

During the socialization period wolf pups become increasingly mobile and playful, often wrestling and chasing one another in strength- and coordination-building exercises. They learn that bashing into a sibling from the side is more likely to knock it from its feet than attacking from the front. Skills such as these not only prepare the pups to interact (perhaps aggressively) with members of their own kind, but also serve as training for hunting as adults.

The final stage of development for wolf pups is the *juvenile stage,* which lasts from twelve weeks until the youngsters become adults. At around three months of age, young wolves begin chasing small creatures such as grasshoppers and mice. They also learn to leap and pounce in an attempt to capture small rodents. Sometime, at about three to four months of age, they may accompany adult wolves on a hunt. However, it takes some time

Most wolves leave the pack to find their own territories before they reach three years of age. Lisa Densmore

for pups to become aggressive toward prey. At first they might be scared of the animals they're supposed to attack. A researcher on Ellesmere Island, a Canadian island near Greenland, witnessed a litter of pups accompanying the alpha male from a pack of arctic wolves as it caught and killed an arctic hare. Rather than rushing

ISSUES & WOLVES

WHY ARE PUPS BORN IN SPRING?

From tiny Chihuahuas to massive mastiffs, all domestic dogs are descendants of wolves. Yet one intriguing aspect of the two creatures' natural history sets them apart: Dogs are able to breed and produce young at any time during the year, while wolves only mate in late winter, with their offspring born in the early spring. What accounts for the difference?

For puppies born in a kennel, their mother is fed plenty of dog food, affording them a steady milk supply as they grow. Once they begin eating solid food, an obliging human provides enough puppy chow to keep them growing and healthy. The situation is much more complex for wolf pups. Their mother needs the pack to provide food to supply her nutritional needs while she nurses her pups. As they transition from milk to meat, young wolves are dependent on the pack for their food.

Wolf pups are born several weeks prior to the birthing time of most of their ungulate prey. About the time the pups begin eating solid food, the pack is able to prey upon baby ungulates, which represent easily catchable prey. Thus, the birth and development of wolf pups coincides uncannily with this windfall in the prey base, increasing their odds of health and survival. Most experts feel this is the reason that wolves, unlike dogs, only mate and produce litters in the spring.

over to investigate the meal, the pups were so frightened by the dying wails of the hare that they took cover in a nearby rock pile.

Although wolf pups will continue to grow after four months, by this time they are fully capable of following the pack as it moves and hunts. For the next several months they will hone their hunting skills as members of the pack. Some young wolves will remain with the pack for up to three years, while others may disperse to find their own territories as early as nine months of age.

CHAPTER 6 Wolves and Humans

Wolves in History

World Cultures

Since prehistoric times, the relationship between humans and wolves has been chronicled in artwork and legend. Paintings from caves indicate prehistoric artists were inspired by wolves, along with numerous other creatures. Roman folklore recounts the story of Romulus and Remus, the founders of Rome. According to the legend, the twin baby boys were ordered to be executed. Instead, the executioner, a servant, left them in a cradle on the banks of the Tiber River. A flood ferried the cradle downstream. The infants were discovered and reared by a female wolf. From this legend came the Lupercalia Festival, or "Wolf Festival." The she-wolf who nursed Romulus and Remus was named Lupa. The festival occurred in the spring and was thought to bring fertility and health to the celebrants.

Norse mythology recounts the tale of Fenrir, a monstrous creature in the form of a wolf. The gods feared Fenrir, so they put him in chains. The immense wolf creature easily broke the chains. The gods conferred with the dwarves who made magic ribbons of six mysterious elements. When the gods challenged Fenrir's strength against the wispy ribbons, he ignored the challenge, saying there was no pride in breaking such feeble bonds. Fenrir agreed to the test, only if one of the gods would place a hand in his mouth. Tyr, the god of war, finally accepted Fenrir's condition. Discovering he couldn't free himself from the magic cords, Fenrir bit off Tyr's hand. One day, predicts the legend, Fenrir will finally break free. He will pursue and kill Odin, the father of the gods. Fenrir will then die at the hand of Vadir, Odin's son.

Wolves have been characters in the legends and religions of other various peoples at different periods in history. Sometimes wolves have been portrayed positively. At other times they have

Wolves have been the subject of human folklore and legends since ancient times.
KEVIN RHOADES

been viewed quite negatively. In Turkish tradition, a mother wolf, Ashina Tuwu, rescued an injured boy. They later had ten half-wolf, half-human children. Bumin Khayan, the oldest of their offspring, became the ruler of the Turkish tribes. Turkish culture still generally regards the wolf as a positive symbol of leadership.

Gaelic mythology from Scotland and Ireland includes legends of Cailleach, sometimes referred to as "the hag," or queen of winter. She works to keep spring from coming and prolong the cold and hardship of winter. Cailleach can take the form of a wolf.

Some traditions assert she summons fierce wolf storms in the middle of January when the days lengthen, indicating spring is on its way. These storms coincide with the coldest portion of winter. One line of Cailleach lore recounts a story similar to Groundhog Day that occurs on February 2. If the first day of February is sunny, Cailleach has fine weather for gathering firewood, which means she can keep herself warm for more nights and winter will be longer. If February 1 is cloudy, Cailleach sleeps and will run out of firewood soon, resulting in a shorter winter. Along with taking the shape of a wolf and unleashing wolf storms on the world, the feared Cailleach is sometimes portrayed as riding on a wolf, bringing destruction and death to people in the darkness and cold of winter.

Native Peoples of North America

Like other peoples of the world, the native peoples of North America did not universally view the wolf positively or negatively. Wolves were held in esteem by many tribes for their hunting skills and intelligence. The Cherokee, Chippewa, Algonquin, and several other tribes had clans known as the Wolf Clan. Wolves were thought to be "medicine" animals by numerous tribes, creatures capable of giving special powers to humans. Indian names often included wolves, suggesting a positive link between the person and the presumed spiritual power of the creature. Nonetheless, wolves were killed through trapping and hunting by many of the North American native peoples. Wolf skins might be worn as ceremonial decorations. Scouts from tribes inhabiting the Great Plains often wore wolf skins. In their sign language, *scout* and *wolf* were the same. Young hunters and warriors were encouraged to mimic the habits of hunting wolves, such as being aware of potential danger behind them and not solely focusing on what was ahead.

The Nunamiut people of central Alaska believed wolves were exceptional hunters from which human hunters could learn much. They were also skillful hunters of wolves. Nunamiut hunters would lure wolves by howling or creeping up on them as they slept.

Native peoples sometimes used the alertness and skills of hunting wolves as models for their own hunting activities. Lisa Densmore

They also devised various traps for wolves, including snares and deadfalls. Deadfalls are a type of trap in which a heavy object such as a log is held in place by a support connected to some type of trigger. When an animal trips the trigger by accidentally coming into contact with it or purposefully taking an attached bait, the "deadfall" drops and kills the creature. Nunamiut hunters, while very skilled in taking wolves, refrained from bragging about their accomplishments. Such activity was thought to bring bad luck. The Nunamiuts did not fear wolves, but they took precautions to prevent wolf attacks.

The oral history of some Athabascan tribes of Alaska and western Canada indicates they deliberately killed wolves (primarily pups at den sites) to decrease predation upon the big game animals the Indians relied on for food.

European Settlers in North America

European settlers in North America took a dim view of wolves. The animals not only proved a perceived threat to human life and livestock, but they were also vilified in certain religious traditions. Sparse biblical references attribute negative wolflike characteristics to evil people, yet the Bible does not judge the creatures evil themselves. Nonetheless certain Christian traditions eventually condemned wolves as animals with an evil nature. Wolves were thought to be gluttonous and cruel. Early immigrants to North America brought with them these negative perceptions. Coupled with real and imagined dangers to people and livestock, these notions inspired settlers with a strong motivation to rid their world of wolves.

As early as 1630, colonists and Indians were offered incentives in cash or commodities to kill wolves. In the early to mid 1800s, many states developed bounty systems for wolf extermination. States paid a cash bounty to residents who brought in hides or carcasses as proof of eliminating a wolf. During the mid to late 1800s, market hunters wiped out extensive herds of bison and elk on the Great Plains and across the West. These vast herds were replaced with domestic livestock. Attacks on cattle and sheep prompted intense government-sponsored efforts to eliminate wolves. The federal government created a division of Predator and Rodent Control within the Bureau of Biological Survey in 1915. Part of this agency's charge was ridding Bureau of Land Management and National Forest lands of wolves. Other predators were targeted as well. Both the public and most professional biologists welcomed these predator suppression efforts. Even in Yellowstone National Park, a refuge created in part for the protection of wildlife, wolf extermination efforts were pursued with enthusiasm. With the exceptions of northern Minnesota and Wisconsin, wolves were essentially eliminated from the contiguous United States by 1940. The 1960s probably

These wolf pups were captured in Yellowstone National Park in 1922. The US government pursued an aggressive policy of wolf elimination from public lands during this era.
COURTESY NPS

represent the low point in wolf numbers in North America in recorded history.

Wolves in Modern Times

As early as the 1940s, a handful of conservationists suggested wolves should be restored to Yellowstone National Park. Among these was Aldo Leopold, considered by many to be the "father" of modern conservation and wildlife management in the United States. An avid hunter, Leopold recognized the value of wolves as creatures and to ecosystems. In subsequent decades field studies of wolves in Alaska, Canada, and Isle Royale provided more objective information about the creatures than most biological treatments of the past.

The 1970s advanced gray wolf conservation on several fronts. Both the gray wolf population in the Great Lakes region and Mexican wolves received protection under the Endangered Species Act (ESA). Gray wolves were listed under the ESA in 1974 and Mexican wolves in 1976, with several revisions and reclassifications that expanded wolf protection under the ESA to all the contiguous United States by 1978. From 1978 to 1982, recovery plans were developed for wolves in the Great Lakes area, the northern Rocky Mountains, and the Southwest. Wolves also took a hand in recovery. Animals from Canada began moving southward in the 1980s. Wolves denned in Glacier National Park in 1986. This fledgling population grew quickly, expanding the range of wolves southward into other parts of Montana in the subsequent decade.

Wolves captured in Canada were transplanted to Yellowstone National Park in 1995.
LuRay Parker, courtesy USFWS

After several years of controversy, wolves were reintroduced to Yellowstone National Park and central Idaho in 1995 and 1996.

These populations encountered an abundant prey base and grew rapidly. By 2002 wolves had exceeded the recovery goal of thirty breeding pairs and 300 animals in Montana, Idaho, and Wyoming set by the US Fish & Wildlife Service (USFWS) that would allow them to be removed from the endangered species list in these states. However, repeated legal challenges by environmental groups and other legal maneuvering forestalled the "delisting" of wolves until 2011, when Congress intervened directly to remove the animals from federal protection in Montana and Idaho and transferred their management to the states. At the time of this delisting, the USFWS estimated a minimum population of 1,700

In the past decade wolf populations have grown substantially in the contiguous United States. YELLOWSTONE NATIONAL PARK

wolves and one hundred breeding pairs in Montana, Wyoming, and Idaho. Gray wolf populations are healthy in Alaska and Canada, where the animals are often hunted as a game animal.

Current Interactions and Challenges

Despite the overwhelming success of recovery efforts in the contiguous United States, gray wolves remain a controversial species whose presence and protection evoke extreme emotional reactions from certain segments of the human population. Many ranchers hold extremely hostile attitudes toward wolves and their actual and perceived threats to livestock. Viewed on a national scale, wolf depredation comprises a small percentage of livestock losses in comparison to other factors such as disease and natural disasters. However, livestock depredation, according to the USFWS, may substantially impact individual ranchers. For example, cattle reared as breeding stock represent an asset worth thousands of dollars per animal. As such, wolf losses represent far more than an incidental cost to livestock producers in some areas.

Some hunters also harbor excessive ill will toward wolves, blaming them for any imagined or real decrease in big-game populations. Most biologists believe wolf predation can locally decrease the numbers of such species as elk, moose, caribou, and deer. In and around Yellowstone National Park, rising wolf numbers have coincided with substantially decreased elk numbers. Although the latest addition to the predation and habitat equation in portions of the contiguous United States (along with other predators, hunting, drought, habitat quality and winter severity), wolves are simply one of a myriad of factors that affect big-game populations.

The "wolf haters'" extreme and often unfounded emotional reactions toward wolves are mirrored as strongly on the opposite side by the "wolf lovers." An intense period of public involvement over several years resulted in the Environmental Impact Statement (EIS) that charted the course for wolf reintroduction to the northern Rocky Mountains. Specific recovery goals, viewed by many as essentially a contract between the federal government and local residents most affected by wolf populations, was developed. However, long after the recovery goals were met, wolf advocacy groups fought their delisting under the ESA. Many of these groups vocally opposed wolf hunting seasons enacted in Montana and Idaho in 2011, attempting to sway the public into believing wolf hunting threatened the entire population. However, leading wolf biologists report wolf populations can normally experience 30 to 50 percent mortality per year without significant declines to the population. States are required to manage wolves in such a way that their numbers do not dip below federal requirements that would trigger relisting under the ESA.

Looking forward it seems reasonable to predict that wolves will continue to expand their range in the contiguous United States, particularly in remote regions of the southern Rocky Mountains and the Pacific Northwest. Like most wolf biologists and researchers, I hope citizens of the United States will develop a more balanced view of the wolf. Wolves are intriguing apex predators, carnivores that deserve no greater or less respect and protection than other species of wildlife. The natural world and human society are healthiest when we view them as such.

Index

Italicized page references indicate illustrations.

About the Author

A writer, photographer, and naturalist, Jack Ballard is a frequent contributor to numerous regional and national publications. He covers a variety of outdoor, conservation, and wildlife topics. He has written hundreds of articles on wildlife-related topics, appearing in such magazines as *Colorado Outdoors, Camping Life, Wyoming Wildlife,* and many others. Ballard also blogs on wildlife topics for Audubon Guides.

Ballard's photos have been published in numerous books (Smithsonian Press, Heinemann Library, and so on), calendars, and magazines. He has received multiple awards for his writing and photography from the Outdoor Writers Association of America and other professional organizations. He holds two master's degrees and is an accomplished public speaker, entertaining students, conference attendees, and recreation/conservation groups with his compelling narratives. When not wandering the backcountry, Ballard hangs his hat in Red Lodge, Montana. See more of his work at jackballard.com.